TERMINAL
CANCER

THE FIGHT, THE DYING,
&
THE AFTERMATH

LAURA KATHLEEN MESA

Copyright © 2022 Laura Kate Mesa

Introduction

If you're reading this book, you or someone you know has been impacted by a diagnosis of terminal cancer. First, let me say that I am sorry you're faced with this dramatic shock in your life. I hope to shed light on this journey by sharing what it was like for my husband and our family. This book addresses our journey from diagnosis all the way to where I am now, in the aftermath of terminal cancer.

The main objective of this book is to open the curtain to a life you never thought you'd be living. Why would you want to open the curtain? Because fear of the unknown is crippling, at times more crippling than the cancer itself. I hope that in sharing our story, the shock effect will hold less power. In this book, you will read about topics that most people don't talk about.

There is a profound lesson in losing control, a beauty that exists in pain, and an eager hope that lives after loss.

Table of Contents

THE FIGHT

Chapter One
Diagnosis

It was May 2020, Kobe had been killed in a helicopter crash five months earlier, a global pandemic had ravished the world, I was graduating from college, and my husband was told he was going to die soon.

In April of 2020, I remember Larry saying that he felt as if there was a weight on his chest. It would sort of come and go but never fully go. We couldn't figure out what was going on with his health; he rarely got sick, and whatever he had wasn't going away. We started feeling a little bit concerned.

For a few weeks, we tried to figure out on our own why he was sick. Finally, Larry went to a doctor who performed some lab tests. They checked his cholesterol levels and white blood cell count, did a D-Dimer test, checked for Valley Fever, and ordered a chest x-ray.

In the weeks leading up to the first doctor's exam, Larry increasingly complained of pain in his calves. The first complaint I can recall was after one of our fun-filled bike rides. We loved to ride our bikes together in the beautiful oak tree neighborhood where we had just purchased our dream home, a 1928 Spanish-style Tudor house in "The Oaks" of Santa Paula, Ca.

There he was on his bike; arms up and stretched out to his sides, flowing freely in the air, and with his head looking up to the sky, and his feet off the pedals, he soared down the hilly street in front of me. I watched him...I mean, I really watched him! I soaked up that moment as if there was something in front of me that required me to remember it. A moment that was more than a moment; a moment in time that served as a gift to us both. I was riding my bike behind him at a slower pace on purpose. I had a huge smile on my face. I was smiling because I was observing my love living life to the fullest. No work, no worries, and no stress; just a hill, two bikes, the wind, and a woman behind him, admiring his childlike joy. It was perfection. When we returned home, Larry began rubbing his calves and said… "It's strange; my calves are so sore." From then on, his calves would get more painful throughout the diagnosis process.

We needed to get the (ordered) chest x-ray at a radiology clinic nearby. When we arrived at the clinic, his calves hurt so much that he stayed in the car, and I went inside. I wrote his name on a clipboard for the first time of what would be many; "Larry Mesa-10/26/1963- 8am." Due to Covid, we had to wait outside for his name to be called via text message. As we waited, we began talking about what the diagnosis possibilities might be. Valley Fever is very common in our area. The doctor thought it COULD be Valley Fever. We were hoping it wasn't, rather just some mild lingering infection. We spoke of our relief that it wasn't Covid. While waiting, our family doctor called and said, "I received your D-Dimer blood test results, and it's very high; you need to get to the emergency room right now." I thought it was his heart. I became anxious and remembered telling him, "We can't go to the nearest hospital because they may not be equipped to help you.", so we drove about 15 minutes longer to arrive at Los Robles Hospital in Thousand Oaks, CA.

I couldn't go into the ER with him due to Covid, so we checked him into the hospital at the entrance door, and I waited outside. An hour went by before he texted me, saying, "They did a chest x-ray, and they saw a nodule, so they want to run some more tests." I'm now sitting in my car, in the parking garage, just listening to music and asking… "A nodule?" I had no idea what a "nodule" was or why it was important. I asked him if I should wait, and if so, I needed to leave to find a restroom; The hospital won't let me in to use theirs. He said he wasn't sure what to expect next, so I should go find a restroom somewhere and come back. Finally, I found a restroom at a local grocery store and then drove back to the hospital parking garage. There I sat, waiting for his next text message. "Baby, they need to run more tests and are admitting me into the hospital, so go ahead and go home, and I'll text you once I know more." A little shell-shocked and confused, I drove home alone, and there I waited, waited, and waited some more. Waiting would be a huge part of our lives going forward.

While in the hospital, Larry had several more tests, including a CT, an MRI, upper and lower endoscopies, chest x-rays, and many lab tests. One of the tests revealed major discoloration on his liver. The discoloration looked like spots, spots that could be cancer. I believe the term they used on one of the written results was "innumerable amount of liver masses are present". That's when I learned that the word "spots" was equal to the word "masses". Later, we learned that they were looking for a primary source of cancer because it wasn't the liver. Those masses came from somewhere else. The primary cancer was likely that nodule they found on his lung a day earlier, but they had to look at everything. The doctors took a second look at the lungs. Could that little nodule seen on the chest x-ray cause his liver to be discolored that much? They covered all their bases; checked his pancreas; it looked fine. Then back to the lungs again. Finally, after scanning the liver again and running more blood tests, they determined that he had primary lung cancer that had spread massively throughout his lymphatic system, into his liver, lymph nodes, and spinal column. That last sentence still shocks me to write and read. We want to go back to the Valley Fever option that we were so concerned about the day before.

Larry sat in his hospital bed alone as the doctors revealed to him that he had stage four, terminal lung cancer. He told them that if I couldn't come in to be with him, he would get me on FaceTime, and the doctor could tell me the devastating news that way. He called me and said, "the doctor wants to speak with both of us." I didn't find out until much later that he had already heard the news. The call was scheduled. I prepared by having a support system with me. My son, his fiancé, and my sister were there with me, ready to comfort me when the news blew through my soul.

I clearly remember seeing the doctor's face on my phone as Larry held his cell phone up, pointing my face towards the doctor's face while lying in his hospital bed. The doctor said, "This is very serious; we don't just keep people in the hospital if it's not serious." I asked what the diagnosis was, and he said, "he has terminal lung cancer, and there is no cure." I was standing in our living room; my son and his fiancé were sitting on the sofa to my right, listening to the call. My sister was sitting there in my living room chair, wearing a navy-blue ball cap and sweatshirt. She had her hands resting on her chin and a frown on her face; they were my support system, and because of them, unlike Larry, I was not alone when I learned that cancer, like shrapnel, would blow through our lives in the coming months, ripping apart the life we had worked hard to build. It was a moment I will never forget; The doctor said the words "terminal cancer," and I instantly clinched my jaw as tight as I could. My first emotion was anger. When he finished telling us this news and walked out of the room, Larry and I talked privately. We agreed that we would wait on the official biopsy results before we accepted the full impact of this diagnosis. He had gone through every test, including a biopsy, but those results hadn't been returned yet.

Anxious to leave the hospital, Larry couldn't wait for them to deal with the issue that brought us to the hospital, the blood clots in his legs. Blood clots, you see, make a D-dimer blood test read high. But for my husband, a terminal cancer diagnosis took precedence in his mind and apparently in the mind of the hospital staff. They never looked at long-term treatment for his blood clots during this visit. They gave him injections for the clots while in the hospital but never gave him a blood thinner prescription. Four days after taking him into the emergency room, he asked me to pick him up. Could anyone blame him for being anxious to come home? He needed emotional support desperately, and the Covid policy was making that impossible.

The date was May 22, 2020. I picked up my husband and brought him home, where we later received a call from the hospital; the biopsy confirmed his diagnosis. His prognosis was 6 months to two years. There we were, laying in our bed together, holding hands tightly, and taking in that blast of news as one flesh. While holding on tightly to each other and our faith, we prayed for help.

Chapter Two
The Telling

We knew we were gonna need help. That meant we'd have to share this information with everyone we knew. It's humbling, you know? To be doing so well in your life one month, then suddenly realizing… life as you know it is about to crumble. Going from helping others to being the ones who need help from others. Having faith that people will step up…well… is humbling.

We started the telling process with our siblings and children. Every time we told someone…it was like reliving the diagnosis process all over again. We didn't know it would feel that way; we learned it felt that way. It's exhausting to tell people the story and then, thirty minutes later, tell it again. Over and over again, we shared that we were facing a terminal cancer diagnosis. When I say "we were facing," I mean just that. When I married the love of my life in 2015, we became united as one. Our marriage vows were "in sickness and in health". We always took our vows seriously.

Over and over again, we cried *after* telling people that Larry had been diagnosed with terminal cancer. Every time we told it, we waited to hang up the phone or for visitors to leave before crying ourselves. We knew that if we cried while telling the news that it would add pain to the ones we were telling.

The hardest telling of all was telling the kids. We scheduled a meeting with Larry's children (my stepchildren). We had to tell them that their dad was diagnosed with cancer and has been given (maybe) two years to live. We asked them if they'd meet us in a park located in the San Fernando Valley; I can still see them slowly walking up to us. There were people all around enjoying freshly cut green grass, tall, beautiful trees, the blue sky, and soccer balls were being kicked around. Life, for all these people, seemed so good, and I was sitting on the grass, doing my best not to cry for what it about to unfold. As they walked up to us, Larry hugged them gently, and we all sat down. After some small talk, he said, "I have some hard news to tell you. I was diagnosed with stage four lung cancer, and it doesn't look good for me. The doctors say I have six months to two years." There was silence, and I spoke up and said… "the doctors say it's terminal." And then I put my head in my hands, and some tears streamed down my cheeks. I remember saying, "I can't do this." Telling these two beautiful young adults this news was extremely difficult. They took it very hard, obviously, but also, I think they were in shock. The gravity of the diagnosis was hard for all of us to wrap our brains around; it was too surreal. Suddenly, we all became smaller in the grand scheme of our very existence in the world. Once we were faced with losing him, everything changed. For me, my mortality seemed intertwined with the one I was "one flesh" with, and therefore, part of me had become terminal too. Cancer seemed to be taking over our lives.

After we told the kids, telling everyone else began. After a while, the telling became too painful and so incredibly exhausting.

Two weeks after Larry's diagnosis, I got a call from a dear friend; she gave me great advice for our new path. Lisa, whose husband had been through a critical cancer battle, told me to choose one person whom I trusted and have that person share any and all news updates going forward. That person would provide updates and information so that neither Larry nor I had to relive everything as the journey progressed. I chose a couple of people to send email updates throughout the cancer process. The only personal updates I/we provided were to our immediate family. This helped a great deal.

Chapter Three
Defragmentation

We began selling our belongings online. One by one, strangers and neighbors would come to our house and buy our "stuff"; appliances, the outdoor tables that we built together, various furniture items, file cabinets, and the red and yellow rose bushes that he got me for Mother's Day just one year ago; it was hard to see everything go. It was as if I was watching a computerized, defragmentation of our existence; each item taken away represented one pixel, and in slow motion, each piece was whisked away, removing the life we had built, a life we loved and appreciated.

I took the sports car that Larry gifted me for my fiftieth birthday and traded it in for a smooth-riding Kia Sorento. Riding in a low-sitting sports car was too painful on his aching body, but it was the only vehicle we had since Larry used a work van for his job. A member of our church family helped fund the cost of a newer SUV, and in doing so, eased Larry's commuting pain. We had a giant estate sale where we sold nearly all our possessions. Many came to help us sell our belongings; church family, friends, my sister, her husband, and my son all stepped up. We eventually sold our house and moved into an apartment about an hour away in Simi Valley, but this allowed us to be closer to family, church, and doctors. Our church actually paid for a moving company, making the move less stressful. Thankfully, our church was pivotal in helping us with anything we needed during this time period.

Transitioning from being a dedicated man in the workforce and me, a college student, on the verge of graduation, to focusing on selling most of our belongings was our new job and our primary focus. Accepting our new path became easier due to the help from our friends, family, and church. There was so much work to do, but we never did it alone. At times, we literally felt carried. Money poured in, labor efforts were provided, and food and supplies were all provided. Whatever we needed, it was provided. What an incredible support system we had. Our hearts were full of gratitude. We learned that gratitude made our burdens easier to carry.

Chapter Four
Attitude

Attitude is almost everything. An attitude of gratitude seems like such a trite phrase, but it's truly what we fell back on whenever our grief hits. I can recall a day while we were living in our apartment in Simi Valley; Larry came into our bedroom and said, "I've been sitting in the living room crying for thirty minutes." I couldn't believe he would wait thirty minutes before coming to get me, but he didn't want to bother me while I was resting. I said, "Babe, you never have to cry alone." That was meant to be a supportive statement, but after some time passed, we both realized that crying alone was something we would both do from time to time. We had to accept that tears were going to be a part of this…a necessary part.

Gratitude is what we talked about that day and the many days ahead. However, tears and gratitude existed simultaneously. One afternoon, Larry said to me, "You didn't sign up for this!" I answered, "Yes, babe, I did. God did not bring us together only for you to support me in my education and help me with my Lupus struggles. God also brought us together for me to be by your side through everything, and none of this is a surprise to Him." We held each other and felt grateful that we had one another, two people who would never leave each other willingly.

For 8 1/2 years, we walked together. For the final 14 months of our marriage, I was charged with the honor of carrying my husband into the presence of the Lord. By the grace of God, we both traveled this path with vigilance, grace, and patience. Attributes which I had to grow in as the journey progressed, but I'd say attributes that Larry already had when I met him. Just by being himself, Larry taught me how to walk him Home with grace and mercy.

I had one person who kept telling me that I was the right person for him "during this time", but in my mind, I'd always respond, "I've been the right one for him for the entire 8 1/2 years that we've built this life. Cancer doesn't get to define our relationship in its entirety, and it doesn't get to define anyone's life in its entirety. Our lives are far more than the cancer days, weeks, months, or years we had left. We couldn't let cancer define the whole of our existence.

Facing the truth of what was happening to us was accepted in an ebb and flow, if you will. It came and went. The idea of something being surreal is the idea of reality being too much to fully grasp. It's safe to say that sometimes we felt the truth of this diagnosis, and sometimes we did what everyone said and "lived in the moment", forgetting that the shadow of cancer was looming. Sometimes, however, it's difficult to live in a good moment; a moment where smiles are abundant, and laughter is present. Sometimes, cancer slaps the concept of "living in the moment" right off your face. It did that to us several times. One minute we would just try to smile and live in the moment; looking at each other, laughing, joking, or watching a movie, and then in the next moment, we were on our way to the hospital because he had a fever, a fever that turned out to be serious enough that a blood transfusion was required. That's what I call a "cancer slap". It happened more often towards the end of his life, but it happened, in hindsight, even before we knew he had cancer. An example would be when those blood clots stopped our ability to take bike rides, or him being so tired at work that he had to sleep during the day...every day. Cancer slapped us around quite a bit. It was our attitude that helped us fight with dignity and grace. But it was the people who reached out and gave their time, money, talent, and prayers who helped us have an "attitude of gratitude".

Often, the best way for us to get attitude adjustments was to listen to sermons or read books together, and sometimes we even sang worship songs together while lying in bed. We had date nights which consisted of me drawing sketches and him creating music on his computer. We prayed together and we always found reasons to laugh. We made fun of cancer, and we found that putting a humor spin on cancer gave it less power over us. We made all kinds of inappropriate jokes about cancer, living, and dying. We laughed in the face of cancer, and the weight our hearts carried became lighter.

Chapter Five
Treatment

Larry and I were presented with several treatment options on this journey. The first treatment consisted of a host of vitamins; these vitamins promoted a healthy liver and immune system. Vitamins such as 50,000mg of vitamin D3, 1000 IU of vitamin E, 1600mg of vitamin C, 1000mg of milk thistle extract, and a few others. He also began the daunting treatment of Rick Simpson Oil (RSO). Rick Simpson Oil is a potent marijuana oil that is administered in very high doses. Finally, a once-a-day pill was prescribed by the oncologist. Larry was diligent in trying all of these treatment options. Obviously, the hope was that they would cure him or extend his life as much as possible. Maybe they worked for a while, and maybe they didn't, but we tried *nearly* everything to give him more time on this earth.

When someone is diagnosed with this type of cancer, they obtain (or should obtain) what is called a "bio-marker" test to understand the genetics of their specific cancer cells. When we got the results of his bio-marker test, we learned that he was positive for the EGFR and PD-L1 marker; this was great news because it qualified him for the "targeted therapy" pill mentioned above.

There are various therapies nowadays; Larry's targeted therapy was a once-a-day pill called Tagrisso or Osimertinib. This drug allowed us to take four road trips together. Because it was only a pill, it made the first six months after diagnosis doable. We were able to enjoy life together outside of hospitals and doctor's offices. In other words, no chemo, no immunotherapy, and no need to be in the hospital. We were so grateful and so hopeful.

Make sure you trust and love your oncologist. Some people don't realize that if you're not comfortable with your oncologist, you have the right to find one you *are* comfortable with. We were not satisfied with the oncologist who diagnosed him while in the hospital. This doctor often dismissed our questions and talked over us when we visited with him. We decided to seek a new oncologist. Through prayer and reaching out to friends and family, Larry received a text message from a colleague at work who said he was "friends with a renowned oncologist at UCLA Medical". We made an appointment right away at UCLA. The new doctor sat down, looked us square in the eyes, and said, "first of all, I am sorry you are here." He was not rushed, and he had a calm demeanor. This doctor was gentle and hopeful. We needed "hopeful". Our new doctor became a giant part of our journey that day. I honestly don't know how we could have gotten through everything we did without him. He agreed that Larry was on the correct targeted therapy; but disagreed that Larry was not a candidate for chemotherapy, and other treatment options, which the original oncologist had advised.

After about four months of doing the Tagrisso pill, it stopped working. The next phase of treatment that we were introduced to was called immunotherapy. Immunotherapy, we thought, would be easier than chemotherapy, as far as side effects. The fact is, Larry got sicker on a couple of the immunotherapy drugs than he did on the chemotherapy drugs.

In time, he began coughing up blood. This introduced us to surgical treatments. Larry had to have a large tumor in his lung cauterized, as a stint was inserted through the tumor, allowing him to breathe easier. To better understand this, it's helpful to know where that primary nodule/tumor was located; the tumor was in the right upper lung and had grown into the bronchial tube, obstructing part of his airway. This surgery was performed by the best pulmonary surgeon at Cedars Sinai Medical. A bronchoscopy was performed, and then a couple of months later, a procedure called Photofrin Laser Therapy was done. This treatment injected his body with a chemical that made him highly sensitive to light but well worth it. This treatment is used to zap cancer cells that obstruct the airway; it has been helpful in some patients with Non-Small Cell Lung Cancer. For two months after this treatment, Larry had to be completely covered and out of any sort of light; He was now photosensitive, but he could breathe much easier. Due to the zapping of the cancer cells, he began coughing up brownish chunks of tissue that had been burnt in the laser treatment. The coughing up of tissue became a part of his daily routine until his passing. Coughing, for the purpose of clearing his lungs from congestion, made him more comfortable. Next, he was given breathing treatments using a machine, which he was able to perform successfully at home.

A combination of chemotherapy and immunotherapy was next. Unfortunately, the chemo drugs were hard on his system, and all in all, he required three blood transfusions to overcome the effects of the chemotherapy. After a few rounds of chemotherapy, his platelets would drop very low, which would require a blood transfusion to bring them back up. If you or your loved one are using a port or passport, the nurses CAN use the port for the blood transfusions, but often, if they are admitted to a non-cancer floor, the nurses are not trained in the use of ports. This happened to Larry. The nurse, not trained in port care, administered the blood transfusion through a vein in his arm; it hurt him quite a bit. Because of that, I pushed to transfer him to the cancer floor so that he could be with staff who had the skillset to care for him the way a cancer patient needs to be cared for. We were thankful that they did not argue with us about transferring him.

To recap the fight, using everything possible; Larry endured; RSO, taking large amounts of vitamins, marijuana, targeted therapy in pill form, immunotherapy, Photofrin laser lung surgery, three bronchoscopies, three blood transfusions, four emergency room visits, chemotherapy, combination chemo/immunotherapy, radiation to the spine, power port surgery. At home, he received breathing treatments, 1% Diclofenac cream rubbed on his spine every few hours, IV Toradol for bone cancer pain, IV fluid therapy, pills like Xanax for anxiety, and anti-nausea and pain medications.

Pain management became our number one goal as he got closer to succumbing to cancer. It was always our goal, but eventually, when treatment isn't working, pain management takes the lead.

We used marijuana in varying forms, Xanax, Morphine, Methadone, Dilaudid, Tramadol, Ativan, Toradol IM, Diclofenac cream for the spine, and heating pads. He had regular time intervals of med pain administration. Breakthrough pain meds were used when the regular meds and doses weren't enough. Xanax often worked to stop the vomiting, which came on when he got anxious or had too many visitors. Tylenol was useful (for a while) for bone pain.

Keeping the bowels clean and clear was very important; we used everything possible to ensure his bowels and bladder were working and functioning; doing this kept gastrointestinal pain at bay. Larry was always in control of what medications he took. I was responsible for making sure he had medications available to him.

Chapter Six
The Good Intended

Good Intentions always deserve grace. If you are on this journey, you have been or will be given advice by those intending to do good. I am also giving you some advice; Be gracious, be kind, and see the heart behind the advice, even if it seems ridiculous, selfish, or thoughtless. We heard about every type of holistic medication out there. We heard about how being positive would change the outcome, "so just think positive". We heard about how someone's outcome was changed due to prayers, and so we needed to "ask more people to pray". They mean well. Let it go and move forward with your fight in the way YOU choose to. One thing we always did was say "yes" to all *real* help, financial and otherwise, and we never turned down prayer.

Chapter Seven
Advice in the Fight

If you're not happy with your doctor, change to a doctor you want in this fight. He or she is like the captain, so make sure they are someone you trust...with your life...and your death.

Keep a dry-erase board up where you write down the medications, doses, and times. Keep a journal with the numbers of each doctor, each hospital, and emergency phone numbers. Write down your health insurance information in that journal as well. It's a one-stop information journal; I suggest keeping it organized and easily accessible.

Make medications easily accessible and organized. Take inventory of your medications and supplies, do that often to make sure you never run low or run out. We purchased a small white shelving system that hung on our bedroom wall next to the door. This was good because Larry could get what he needed if I was busy; it also served as a reminder to us constantly of what we had. If it got low, we turned the bottle around until it was replaced, and then we placed it front-facing when it was filled.

Stay <u>ahead of the pain</u> to prevent suffering.

Let him or her do what they feel they can/want to do as far as taking care of themselves. Don't take control. This is living for them. Let them control how it's done. Let them decide who they want to visit and who they don't want to visit; also, how many at a time and when. This is a matter of their own dignity and their own rights. Just help them facilitate their desires.

LAURA KATHLEEN MESA

THE
DYING

Chapter Eight
Acceptance

This is a tough topic. When does someone actually "accept" the fact that they are dying? And when does a spouse actually accept the fact that the love of their life is dying?

Larry didn't accept that he was dying in one fell swoop. He didn't accept it until a couple of months before his passing; even then, he didn't fully accept it until the end was staring us down. For him, it happened in waves. I think, personally, that it was better for him that way. I, on the other hand, accepted it much sooner. After all, I had a job to do. I needed to do every job going forward, none more important than making sure his pain levels were as manageable as possible, a vow I made to him when this all started, a vow that he depended on.

Going from working 60 to 70 hours a week to selling our belongings and relocating was a part of our process. There is a layer of acceptance that takes place with each phase; it was like stripping layers from an onion: The first layer is the diagnosis, then not being able to work, then selling the house, then the car, then moving into an apartment in another city, then no longer being able to take trips, then being bed bound, and on it went; one layer at a time, until full acceptance was reached a week before he passed.

He voiced it out loud three days before his passing; "I guess it's time now, baby?" He finally had all the layers stripped away, and he knew the time had come to go home. The two main outer signals were pretty clear; Edema was the first real physical sign, but it was the swelling of his liver that made us realize that our time together was coming to an end.

As I gave the idea of acceptance a lot of thought for this book,

I came to understand that acceptance is maybe easier when it's left to one's last days or hours. I say that because it allows the one who is dying to better live out the days they have left to live.

Chapter Nine
The Miracle of Immortality

A miracle was what we wanted, what we hoped for. We had a lot of people praying for a miracle. They were praying for healing to take place in my husband's cancer-filled body. We heard it often. Whenever someone said they were praying for a miracle, my mind wondered if they knew that the miracle had already happened. We were thankful for their prayers, their love, and their good intentions. God was speaking to our hearts, though, telling us, "The miracle is already accomplished." God did that on the cross when he conquered death and the grave. Because of that cross and resurrection, we shed these decaying bodies, and we live forever in a place called Heaven.

Many people talk of Heaven and going to a "better place". It's usually talked about at funeral services. We talked about that place often. We wrote about Heaven and sang songs about Heaven; it was always on our minds. Some cancer patients do get better, but many die. It doesn't take away from the miracle of Christ. It doesn't take away from us getting our miracle.

Chapter Ten
Final Visitations

In the final weeks of Larry's life, we strategically planned who would visit him. It's a complicated decision; only the one facing death can decide when and how these visits happen, but the caretaker can (and should) help facilitate the visits. That's how we did it. He said what he wanted, and I worked to make it happen.

I contacted Larry's siblings and two of his cousins. He wanted a chance to say goodbye to them all, so one by one, they came. He couldn't see them all at once because it would overwhelm him. After the siblings and cousins, we scheduled time with his two best friends. Lastly, we scheduled time with each of our children… one at a time.

There was a moment when our older son, Dustin, gave me some powerful advice. Dustin is Larry's stepson and was concerned for Larry's children. His concern was that they would miss an opportunity to say the things that they would want to say if they accepted that their dad was dying. "What do you want him to know if he died tomorrow?" That was how Dustin put it. He said to call Larry's kids and tell them to write a letter or come in person to voice what they want their dad to know. So, I called and/or texted Larry's children and told them exactly that. After calling and texting them, I told Larry the same things; "What do you want your children to know if you were to go home to Heaven tomorrow?" So, Larry took a Xanax and thought about these things before meeting with his kids. This is important because it allows a person to go through their passing without the fear of things left unsaid. It's also critical for the children left behind. It was/is a gift.

Joshua (Larry's son) and Larry sat alone in our bedroom; the door closed. There, they talked for two hours about life and their love for each other. Dustin (my son) got to sit and talk to Larry about how grateful he was that his mom got to meet, marry and have a life with a man like him. Andrea (my daughter), her husband Matt, and our grandkids drove from Oklahoma to visit him one last time; and finally, Erica (his daughter) got to walk alongside her dad; with me on one side and her on the other, we gently took him to his hospital bed which was placed in the dining room a few days before her visit. It was there that she heard him call her "Princess" one last time. These are the people he wanted to see before the quiet hours of his passing began. I look back on it now in great appreciation for these visits, each one holding its own special meaning.

Larry voiced that he didn't want to spend his last few days worrying about me. Responding with an eagerness to soothe his worry, I told him simply, "Okay, Babe, we will focus solely on you going forward." In those last days, I made sure not to cry in front of him, voice concerns about my heartache, the security of my future, or anything else concerning me. I heard him, we looked deeply into one another 's eyes, and I understood what he was saying. He needed to focus on going to Heaven. He was ready. I needed to focus on walking him there in peace. Even if I wasn't ready. After all, I would never be ready.

Chapter Eleven
The Details of Dying

The details of dying from cancer are hard to talk about. This section addresses some difficult issues regarding the dying process. It was not all difficult; some of it was beautiful for us. However, some of it was very difficult as well.

I wish I had known about some of the physical changes that happened beforehand, and that's one of the main reasons for writing this section. I hope they help someone out there to be more prepared than I was: Larry had started turning more jaundice, and the vomiting became more often in the weeks before, but less in the last week. Edema, which is the swelling of hands and feet, became noticeable. When the edema happened, that's when we knew it was time to stop administering IV fluids. Lastly, the section of his upper right belly became hard and was swelling. The swelling in the liver was not super noticeable, but if you really looked, you could see it. The liver failure was painful, but we managed it by keeping him lying down and not bending his torso. For Larry, the liver pain only got severe in the final three days of his life. Keeping him in the prone position and on a Dilaudid pump helped limit his abdominal pain.

I want to go back in time here because we talked with our oncologist a few months before Larry's body began shutting down. We wanted to understand what it looked like, how to prepare if we had options, and what were the medical plans for this part. Our oncologist advised that while California has a legal "aid in dying" law, he didn't typically go that route, but it is Larry's choice. Larry said he didn't want to take the aid-in-dying route but preferred another route, one that allowed him to be as interactive with visitors and as pain-free as possible to the very end; at that point, the doctor said that the hospice company would use a sedative combined with either Methadone, Morphine or Dilaudid in increasing dosages. The purpose of the drugs is to first remove pain, then he would be unconscious; after that, his body would begin shutting down, and finally, while unconscious, he would take his final breath. Working with the hospice company, we chose the Dilaudid pump, which allowed me, as his wife, to help him as he neared the end.

It was helpful to know what his options were ahead of time. Some states do not have aid-in-dying laws, so if you want this option, find out the laws where you are. It is a rigorous option, but for some, it is chosen. In all honesty, it's not much different than assistance using a pain medication combined with a sedative like Xanax or Ativan. It's just different. I can't speak to the differences because we didn't consider the assisted death option.

About two days before his passing, drinking water became very limited. To quench his thirst, he took small sips to start, then ice chips, and then when he went unconscious, I used a moistened swab to dab on his lips, just in case it was bothering him and he couldn't tell me.

Before Larry went unconscious, he stood up to urinate in a urinal because he couldn't make it to the bathroom. He filled the urinal with brownish-colored urine, then he laid back down. That was the last time he used the restroom, and he never soiled the bed, even after passing. The nurse and I helped him stand up that one last time. It was his final independent/dependent action. It meant a lot to him to be able to stand and just pee on his own. For every phase of this illness, it's important to give the dying person their dignity, the right to choose the way *they* want to handle each step, and help them as they want you to.

Let's address palliative and hospice care. To explain the difference in the simplest way, it's like this: palliative care is not end-of-life care; that's hospice care. Hospice helps you get to the end of life, and palliative care helps you go through the illness. You can go on and off hospice as many times as you need to. Disease is not always predictable, so manage your resources wisely. We were told by our second hospice company that we were not allowed to give IV fluids. Larry and I were both very upset about this, so we contacted our oncologist, who said… "They don't want to give you IV fluids because they are given a fixed amount of money each month to care for him, and they don't want to spend it on IV fluids; I'll call." See how having a great oncologist to captain your ship works to your benefit? That second hospice did not want to allow him to have fluids, so we changed for a third time to a company named Vitas. We were not controlled by *their* "wants"; we were instead a team. Larry got his fluids (which gave him great peace), and any other needs he had were taken care of in a timely manner.

There were some beautiful parts to the dying process: Three days before his passing, Larry and I were lying in our bed together. I looked to my left, and there he was, his right arm up and moving from an upward to downward curving motion. To me, he was petting air until he said, "Hi Jax, hi buddy". Jax was our dog, we had gotten him right after getting married, and Jax was put to sleep about a month earlier. I said, "Babe, do you see Jax?" To which he responded with, "No, no, that couldn't be Jax." In hindsight, I would have just been quiet and let him have an uninterrupted experience with our dog.

There were a couple of times when he started looking out and up, as if he was seeing something I couldn't. He told me he was just pulling my leg, but I wonder now. Two days before his passing, he was seeing images in the hallway and asked us to move a coat that was hanging in there, so we did. The day before Larry passed away, he began to drift in and out. The hospice nurse was with us, and she said the words… "He is transitioning." Even though I knew he was progressing towards passing away, I hadn't really accepted that it was happening right then. I was still in "job" mode. I needed to make sure he was at peace; the music I played was calm, scripture was being played from his phone, and he experienced no pain. I think the busy job helped me cope with the fact that I was in the very deep process of losing him. Suddenly, all my busy time was interrupted…I was sitting next to him, on the right side of the bed; Larry said, "Wow, these mirrors are **fantastic**," to which I replied, "I cannot see the mirrors, Babe, but I love the word "fantastic." That was on Wednesday afternoon, July 28th, at 2:22pm; I looked at my watch, looked up to the ceiling, and saw what I can only describe as a prism in the ceiling. It had two protruding pointed sections and a smaller section that was just a prism without a point. The room had blackout shades covering the windows, so no light could get into the window where this presented itself. I clearly remember not wanting the hospice nurse to know what I was seeing. I would look up at it, look back at him, look up at it again… and back at him again. I repeated that three or four times before I realized that this light insisted that I pay attention to it. Not saying anything to the nurse, I nodded my head up and down in a "yes" motion, and it went away. After that, things were calm for about an hour; by calm, I mean no signs of passing away; he simply looked like he was sleeping.

At about 3:30pm on July 28th, Larry started what is called a "death rattle". This is when a person who is completely unconscious builds up fluid in the back of their throat as their physical body begins to shut down. The passing person is not able to swallow due to being unconscious, so the saliva builds up. However, if the body takes a long time to shut down, swallowing can occur due to reflex. Larry also started what is called "agonal breathing". Agonal breathing often happens in lung cancer patients and heart disease patients. Also, agonal breathing usually lasts longer when a person is younger. For Larry, he had a healthy heart and was only 57 years old, so his body took a long time to stop its natural respiration. His body experienced agonal respiration that lasted for 13 hours. He did not respond to my cues or touches at all. I played gospel music that he loved and alternated that with scripture. The next morning, July 29, 2021, at 3:29 am, I watched my love take his final breath. Our home was peaceful. The nurse was scheduled to leave at 4am, so the time that he officially passed away was helpful in that the nurse was there to help me prepare his body to be picked up.

For some reason, I wanted Larry to have on warm sweats, so I asked her to help me change him from shorts to warm sweats, and she did. As we turned his body while dressing him, the fluids that built up in his throat poured out on the bed next to me. He was gone, and it was obvious to me at that point, but I still wanted him to be warm...for me.

Shortly after his passing, my sister drove like a bat out of hell to be with me before they took his body away. Layla (our dog) was lying under Larry's bed when the funeral home employees arrived to take his body. Sadly, Layla began barking; it seemed she did not want them anywhere near Larry. I had to tell them to please go outside and let me get our dog calmed down. Finally, I was able to coax her out from under the hospital bed and into my arms. They came back in, put Larry's body in a bag, and carried him out. At that very second, I looked at my sister, and in my non-Christian, very fleshly existence, I uttered the fine words... "What the FUCK!" And she replied with, "Right?" It was just that kind of moment. It was too much, too surreal, too hard, too painful. My love had left the day before but watching his body leave...I felt cut in half.

Chapter Twelve
A Letter to Jesus

Dear Lord,

Only you can fully understand what we have been through in the past fourteen months. I thank you for the honor of knowing this man, being genuinely loved by him, and finally seeing that I am worthy of a very good man. You've prepared me for hard times, you've put a chant in my heart, and you bring it to the forefront of my mind often. "The hardest things in life are the most rewarding, so do hard things." Lord, this is, by far, the hardest of the hard things I have done. Thank you for your Spirit that resides inside of me. Thank you for the courage to endure the tragedy of cancer. Thank you for the armor that you have so gently put on our souls. We were brave because of you, we were gracious because of you, and we see forever because of you. Now, my Lord, please walk me through the aftermath.

LAURA KATHLEEN MESA

THE
AFTERMATH

Chapter Thirteen
Slow It Down Now

A painful, strategic free fall of faith…that's the best way to describe this part of the journey. I became untethered: untethered from my husband, my identity as a wife, my house, my car, my city, and my church. I became untethered from…my life. The next step was for me to freefall through this thing called grief. And so it goes.

I needed to stay in the place where Larry passed, at least for a few months before my move north. How long you stay in your home is up to you unless finances force you to leave. For me, I wanted to sell everything and run away. I think I lost it for a while…I know I did. Thanks to my family and friends, I stopped selling our stuff. I stopped looking for a new place to live. I took my brother-in-law's offer to stay in that little beach apartment a bit longer. I'm glad I did. That race car that was spinning around in my brain at high speed needed time to slow down. I needed to take care of myself. I was resting more, doing breathing exercises every day, creating art, singing and writing songs, and taking walks. Then I started writing this very cathartic book, and sometimes I did nothing at all. Some days, my only goal was to stay alive.

A couple of weeks into my grief journey, I sat down at the keyboard; I had a strong desire to sing a song that Larry and I wrote together, but as I began singing that song, what poured from my mouth were completely different lyrics. Sitting there at my keyboard, hunched over in ache and exhaustion, I sang new lyrics…. "Slow it down now, won't you just slow it down for me." I sang it over and over again, slowly and calmly, as if it were helping me to do what I was asking for. The lyrics were given to me in that moment; I realized that from the innermost part of my soul, you know the part… it's that place where powerful songs are written;

I was being told that I needed to slow down now. My very heart was telling me to stop and mourn the loss of my husband. I think I needed permission to mourn. I know it might seem strange but giving myself permission helped me to just be there, in grief. I needed to feel everything so much slower than at the pace I was feeling it. I had been working so hard for months, and that work came to a halt. Now, I needed my mind and body to catch up with the reality of my current existence.

When I packed up that little place on the beach, I took a tally of what I had left after the storm of cancer ravished our world. I realized I had lost a lot of things and a lot of non-things, but I hadn't fully lost my mind. I also hadn't lost my faith, my true friends, or my family.

Kathy Lee Gifford was on the Today Show talking about how she stayed in her and Frank's home for six years after he passed away; she said the loneliness was palpable. I related to her when she said that she had to move to a whole new place. Like me, the memories were killing her, and it was time to make new ones. I'd say that is a good way to put it. You sort of simmer in memories after losing a spouse; you simmer and soak in them. What I realized is that those memories needed to become my life jacket, not a weighted vest that I wore in the sea of grief I was swimming in.

Once Larry left the earth: I needed to stop the angst, the worry, and the stress that comes from caring for another human being. It was time to stop trying to be this man's hero because he wasn't here anymore. Now, I needed to try to become my own. What I mean is...I tried to be strong for him, but now I needed to dig deep and be strong for myself. To do this, my focus needed to shift. At times, I couldn't help but feel guilty about caring for myself. I felt guilty if: I sat down for a nice meal, got a massage, spent any money on anything that I didn't need to survive, or just watched television all day. Then I realized it didn't matter what people thought about how I was grieving because no one out there really understood what I had been through; nobody knew but God and my husband; they couldn't.

I know that God wants us to care for ourselves. He sent His angels to walk beside us in our difficult and (occasional) heroic times of caregiving. He has seen it all! So, with that, go ahead and slow it all down now: rest, sleep, exercise, eat well, get a massage, get lost in a movie, go shopping, get those nails done, or go fishing. Whatever it is that helps you get to a calming place, a *healthy place,* and a place of comfort…DO THAT!

Chapter Fourteen
Going Back to Church

I rolled out of bed at 7am. Layla, as always, expects me to take her for her morning walk so she can do her business. I take her out, and as always, her potty time promotes mental wellness for me. I get to walk along the shoreline and even stare at the seals who seem to oddly notice us every single time, singing the awkwardly driven tunes that only seals and sea lions can produce. It was a short walk this morning before heading back to the house. Without hurry, I make a cup of coffee, sit in my chair and look at my text messages and social media accounts. I remembered that it was, in fact, Sunday morning and glanced at my watch. I talk to myself …"You haven't even brushed your teeth; you'd at LEAST have to brush your teeth! Church starts in 30 minutes, and it's 18 minutes away! You don't have time! Make time! You don't have time! Wait until a later service! No, go now! Ugh, stop trying to figure it out! Walk to the bathroom, put a little deodorant on, and go!" So, that's what I did. I told Layla to "stay". I walked out of my front door, un-showered, not a stitch of make-up on, but I DID brush my teeth and slap on some deodorant. I'll just go in, praise God, listen to the message and walk out. No one will even notice me; it's a big(ish) church. I put the address on my phone and off I went wearing Larry's t-shirt and a skort. My legs were unshaven; I'm certain I had chin hairs that hadn't been plucked in way too long and likely still had sleepy gunk in the corner of my eyes, but I guess my desire to worship collectively (yet invisibly) was more important to me than how I looked or how I might be judged by people at this new church.

I drove to the wrong location (stupid smartphone). The conversation I had in my mind was… "It's okay that you got lost; this only means you won't have much time before service starts, which means people won't attempt to approach you. This misnavigation worked in your favor!" I finally made it to the new church, pulled in and parked, grabbed my own water bottle (so I wouldn't have to approach a coffee, water, or social bar if I was thirsty), and walked in. I felt both welcomed and overwhelmed at the same time. No one here knows; no one here knows what my past 14 months have been like; no one here knows that I just lost the greatest man to ever walk the face of the earth or that he was a worship pastor and I'm gonna keep it that way! Self-talk tends to take a back seat when God moves, and boy, did God step in? I walked in, took about 15 steps or so, and on the right wall, it said something about welcoming guests. It had a counter that had a clipboard. There was a man and a woman standing behind the counter. I walked up to that counter as if it was a magnet that I couldn't avoid. My soul knew these were my brothers and sisters. God knew I needed them, and so He drew me to them. I mean, that's God, right?! The man looked at me and said, "You look like you have a question," to which I responded with a summary of my story. It just came out as if I unconsciously needed to share, and by sharing, I was somehow displaying that I needed a hug, a hug that might prevent me from briskly walking back to my car and speeding away. He walked around the counter and asked if he could hug me (Covid rules and maybe some polite gentlemen rules too). He gave me a warm hug and showed me around the place. He even walked me into the sanctuary where I comfortably sat near the back and on the end chair, you know, in case I needed to exit quickly.

As the music started, I found myself comfortable and relaxed. It was dark, so no one could really see how unkempt I was. About thirty minutes into the service, a group came in and sat next to me. Ten minutes later, a man walked in, scooted by my legs, and sat next to the group on my left. I looked over and noticed a familiar face that I hadn't seen in over ten years or so. I looked at him in the dark room, and I knew it was my old friend, Randy. I whispered, "Hi Randy." He looked at me, our eyes locked, and he gave me two brotherly embraces, which was so nice of God to do. After church, he shared that he had weekly dinners at his place, about twenty minutes from where I was living. A connection with brothers and sisters in a new environment. God loves us so much.

Back to the most beautiful thing about my first time back in church. I need to tell you this because it's a critical aspect of healing, coping, and growing. Remember earlier when I said I wanted this to be not so much about me? That's true; it's both true that I wanted to worship and propel my love upwards toward Jesus and praise in a collective setting, but it's also true that God wanted to love on me. Both happened. I was embraced, and the message was just what I needed to hear. Finally, I sat in a church and listened to the messenger talk about how church is about coming together and then going out into our communities. It's about impacting our communities through acts of love. She also said the most beautiful thing, which I think took courage. She said coming to church isn't just about what you can GET from a church or God; it's about what you can GIVE to God while in church, i.e., worship, praise, thanksgiving, honor, glory, and I added to that (in my mind) trust. That's what I needed. I needed the focus not to be on me, my hurt, my pain, my loss, my suffering. I needed to level up, look up and point up! The power of taking the focus off OUR need and suffering and redirecting it to loving our Heavenly Father is profound. In redirecting our thoughts and emotions, we magically find contentment, peace, and hope. Ahhhh, yes, hope. Thank you, Jesus, for loving me and giving me the desire to love you. But also, thank you for hope.

Chapter Fifteen
Signs & Wonders

God, the creator of the universe, gives us gifts in nature: gifts that soothe us and rock our aching hearts to sleep. It's on those days when it feels like our heart will break and shatter on the floor when, if we look for it, He shows us He is there, putting our heart in His hands and keeping it beating. The beautiful things that I experienced after Larry passed away happened in nature. Naturally, God would wrap me up in this way. It's the way I love the most. I kept a diary of cool ways that God presented Himself to me. I hope you too will look and discover signs of your own. In the meantime, I hope my experiences warm your heart and maybe say, "wow!"

A day after Larry passed away, I went for a walk along the ocean's harbor behind our house. As I walked, I noticed a seal swimming in the opposite direction of my walk; it was in the middle of the harbor, swimming alone. As my stride passed the seal, I was compelled to keep looking back at him, and he was swimming slow enough to look back at me and Layla. Eventually, I stopped walking and that seal, swimming in the middle of the harbor, turned and swam to the side where Layla and I were standing. Once he arrived at the shoreline, he came up out of the water, looked me square in the eyes, and went back down before swimming away. I would have questioned if the incident had any real meaning…but a lady on a yellow bike stopped behind me and witnessed it. She said… "Did you see that?… He came up to say hi to you!" I just knew it was a moment for me to hold onto. He was paying attention to me; He was seeing my ache; He was with me.

The next day, about 30 or more seals began mating and congregating on the sandy area behind our house. It had been a very long time since they congregated in that location. I was able to walk over to the seals for weeks after his passing.

Larry passed away on July 29, 2021. One month later, two hurricanes formed in the Atlantic Ocean; their names…Kate and Larry. I believe the headlines read "Kate Persists, Tropical Storm Larry forms" Since my name is Kate and my husband is Larry, I found that extraordinary. From what I understand about the naming of hurricanes, they choose them well ahead of when they hit, but it was interesting because I know God is not limited by time and space like we are. Therefore, I saw it as something to notice. God wanted me to know that Larry was with Him, and they were behind me in this journey, a journey that I often felt I was walking alone.

I saw giant rainbows in foggy skies while driving: their importance for me was in their ability to get me to look up, to stop looking down, to see something bigger than myself, something bigger than my pain. Nature became a sort of superhero for me. Everything in it somehow became more vibrant after my world was drastically altered. I wondered why everything didn't seem dimmer, why more vibrant? I didn't feel vibrant as a human. It didn't make sense unless the one who created it all…was letting me know I would be okay. In my palpable weakness, He would be my strength. One day, the sun seemed to brighten everything it touched, then a few days later, the sun had a new job…it now needed to wake up MY senses to that which it touched. The grass was greener; the ocean white caps were brighter, the sky was a bluer shade of blue, and the rainbows looked to hold more variance of color.

My friend, Shannon, waited to visit me until things had gotten quiet. Once the funeral was over, and people stopped visiting, she flew from Oklahoma City to Santa Barbara. We took a boat to the Channel Islands. The company, "Island Packers", provides daily trips out of the harbor, where Larry and I were living. I've gone on these boat trips several times over the years. While there is a high chance that people will see thousands of dolphins on these boat rides, people rarely get to see dolphins AND whales this time of year. On our trip that day, we saw something never seen by the captain: We saw many dolphins, we saw a whale, and then…there was the awesomeness reserved for us …we saw a shark… not just a shark, but a shark feeding… in the wild! The boat stopped, and we all observed the shark circling its meal and then slowly eating it. The captain got on the mic and told us that in thirty years, she had never seen this type of event on one of these commutes to the islands. I, of course, spoke up and said, "I asked God to let us see the extraordinary today, and He is doing that."

My sister and I took a healing trip to Utah. On this trip, we experienced a couple of cool "signs" that I am excited to share with you. As I was preparing for this trip, I looked up some locations in Zion National Park; places that I wanted to be at for Larry's birthday, which is October 26th. As I was researching locations using my VR headset, I pulled up "Wonder", an app I like to explore on my VR. I noticed on the map of Zion National Park that there was a place called "Great Heart Mesa". As I looked in my VR, I thought it looked very familiar, like maybe it was the place where Larry and I stood together in 2019. We took photos there but never knew the name of the location. Those pictures are hanging on our living room wall. I remember lifting my VR from my eyes to my forehead and then looking at the photo on the wall, back to the VR, back to the wall, several times before realizing… Those pictures were taken at "Great Heart Mesa"! Our last name is MESA! Wow, I thought that was so cool!

On the drive to Utah, my sister and I stopped at Charlie Browns, the famous gift shop and restaurant on Pearblossom Highway in Little Rock, California. It's tradition for us to stop there. As kids, we often stopped there with our dad. While exploring the store, I noticed some birth year plaques. You know the kind…It has the year you were born and something special that happened on that date in history. I was trying to find Larry's year. I found my year, but 1963 seemed to be sold out. I couldn't stop looking for it. It just bothered me that his wasn't there, yet so many others were. After a couple of minutes, my sister walked up to me, and I said, "will you help me find Larry's year, "1963", I found mine, "1966". Then, suddenly, *with my sister watching*, I moved my year to the right, and behind it was 1963, the only one there, and it was hiding behind mine. We both knew instantly that it was a sign…literally.

When my sister and I arrived in Zion, we, of course, stood at "Great Heart Mesa". I, so as not to frighten the other people standing at that spot, informed them that I would be yelling to the Heavens a shout of "Happy Birthday" to my husband, a great man who recently passed from Cancer. Another lady standing nearby told me that she was there celebrating her son's birthday; he had recently passed too. We hugged so tight. And then, with a crackling and broken voice, looking up to the sky, I yelled out, "Happy Birthday, Babe! I miss you!"

I don't go around playing the lottery, but I thought I'd throw my chances out there when the winnings were super high, it was around the end of 2021. I was staying on the Oregon Coast at the time, just exploring the beauty there, so I stopped into a small-town's convenience store (those have the best chances to win… they say). I purchased five tickets! I didn't win the lottery, per se… I sort of DID win, though… and here's why; The winning numbers didn't match my ticket, but the winning numbers were: 12, 22, 66, 54, 69, and 15. My birthday is 12-22-66, and I am 54. The number 69 represents wealth, and the number 15 represents the year Larry and I were married. The message… My financial help comes from the Lord, and I need to trust what Larry set up for me when we got married. I heard it loud and clear. And in the hearing, I won the lottery.

Chapter Sixteen
From Married to Widowed

My husband and I had an entire army behind us while we went through the cancer journey: My daughter set up GoFundMe pages and Google fund raisers, we made cookie sales, and donations of cooked meals were coming in in droves. An entire group of ladies on Facebook (who we didn't know) purchased Christmas gifts for us, our kids, and our dogs; it would be our last Christmas together. There was a mountain of support from what seemed like…well… everyone.

The insanity of how life can be so full one Christmas and so excruciatingly empty the next is a shock to my system. I did not want to be alone for my birthday and my first Christmas without Larry. Instead of being alone, I planned a trip north. Being with my son in Oregon felt exciting to me. It gave me something to look forward to. I needed something to look forward to.

Before I can leave for Oregon, I must endure days and nights of loneliness. Nights when I beg for time to go back two years so I can hold him one more time. My support system had become much smaller than it was when he was here, but it consisted of those who truly loved me. At night, it's just me and my pup, Layla. So much is missing, so very much is missing. Silence wants to become a new friend of mine, but I'm just not sure if I want to let go of the noise. Yes, I am now in a relationship with nouns. There is no one here to have small talk with, no one to have deep, meaningful talks with, no one to have art sessions with. Cancer has silenced me.

When Larry left this earth, all income ceased. When he was here, we received his Social Security checks every month. When he passed away, all income stopped. Larry's brothers, sister, and my dear friend, Kevin, all stepped up for me. They continued looking out for me as far as financial needs.

This might be hard to read, but it's the truth…The idea of "shock giving" is something to think about. We had what I call 'Shock Support". When Larry was diagnosed, and don't get me wrong, we were (and I still am) grateful for it, but once the shock wears off and the cancer patient has been laid to rest, people need to get on with their lives. Nearly all the donations and support go away for most people, and that was no different for me. People could not keep going at the pace they were going while we were battling cancer. The memorial represents closure for many of those who were helping. It's important for you to be ready for this in case it happens to you. Talk about it with your family, friends, and church. If this happens to you, please tell people you feel forgotten about so they can rally around you. The ones who are supposed to…will.

A couple of weeks after Larry's memorial service, I was (and still am) extremely sad, so very lonely, and still so in shock. Sometimes I get anxiety attacks. To describe it metaphorically, it was like this for a while: walking from the living room to the bedroom, I needed to walk down the hallway. As I walk through the hallway, everything starts going in slow motion; it's as if the hallway is housing a cloud of grief. That grief just hangs there, waiting for me to go into the bedroom that I (so recently) shared with my husband. I need to walk through that cloud because it's the only path that leads to our bedroom. I walk through it. It wraps me up like a coat draping around my shoulders, weighing me down, and my spirit is now hunched over. Then, I reach our bed, or is it *my* bed now? I don't know how to reconcile an answer to that one. There, in "our bed", I lay down in this grief coat, and it transforms into my blanket, covering me without my approval. I begin a conversation in my mind that goes like this…."How do I live without you, Babe?" "How do I exist without you?" "How do I breathe without you?" The answer to the question "how?" comes to me. I hear it in my heart, and it goes like this: "Choose to move forward, one weighted step at a time! Trust God, give in to the reality that life as you knew it is gone, you can create a great life, let go of the idea of the impossible, be stronger than you ever thought you could be, play and make music, create art, read books, write books, abide in the one you trust most, Jesus, eat healthy food, believe that you can do hard things, don't look so far in the future that you can't take a step today, but think about the future when you're making decisions, always ask for help! Finally, no matter what...DO. NOT. QUIT!" And with that... I fall asleep.

It's been a few months, but it feels like it's been a few days. I've been living in a twilight-zone existence for months now. It hurts to allow time to go on without him, as if I had a choice. But really...the audacity of time to even think it has the right. I want him back. I don't want him back as a cancer sufferer. I want him back as he was before cancer so rudely introduced itself into our lives, an unwelcomed tornado spinning debris of tears, sweat, blood, and shock into our existence. Here I am, lying in bed on a Monday night, all alone and, yes, lonely. Everyone I know has someone with them, but I am here, alone. My life partner has been ripped away from me without our approval. I am required to make decisions that he used to make. I am expected to figure out how I will manage life without him. Everyone wants to know what I am going to do. I don't know what I am going to do, so I always respond with the same answer, "I don't know."

Today, I couldn't breathe for a while; at least it felt that way. I am lost, I am confused, I am alone. That's how it feels, and it's frightening. It's not fair, and for me...it feels as if the very concept of "love" has found me unworthy of its company. I know better, though...See, the thing is...God *is* love, and He has not abandoned me. A lesson in the difference between feeling and truth. Feelings are fleeting; truth is...well... solid.

It's been four months, six days, and 12 hours since my husband passed away. I'm finally ready to leave the beach apartment we moved into, the place where he wanted to live out his last days. He used to say the air here was perfect. And...it was, but now it's anything but perfect to me. I'm planning on going up to Oregon in a week, finally. I don't know for how long or where exactly I will settle down, but I need to leave this place.

I know I am blessed! I hate that I feel the need to keep telling people that I know I am blessed. Yes, I am grateful...but I don't have to deny the part of our journey (and now my journey) that I hate. I don't have to always say "I am blessed", or "I am grateful." It hurts when people feel the need to remind me how blessed I am when I am talking about how damn hard this is! It is excruciating! I am traumatized by all that terminal cancer put us through, but I know we did it well. I am mad at those who abandoned me after he passed away! But I am thankful for those who stayed. I am so pissed at cancer!!

Chapter Seventeen
Everything Is Different

Understanding what grief looks like on a day-to-day basis is impossible for me to grasp, let alone someone not experiencing it, but this chapter aims to help people gain a little understanding. The hope is that the person grieving, be it you or someone you love, will be kinder, more patient with yourself, or the one you love. Take your time, slow down and take deep breaths. Stop trying to understand fully why things don't make sense and accept that they don't have to. You lived with another person for a long time. Now, everything is different, from what you watch on television to what time you go to bed…everything is different. Learn to live freely in what is now different.

Things happen in life that change a person; He changed me, it changed me, and I am changed. I no longer find significance in the petty things of life. I am not so concerned about what others think of me. As of writing this chapter, I have no idea what my future holds. While I am concerned, my concern is limited to what I now know of time; time here on earth is short. I've spent far too much time believing it was long. "I miss you"; those three words cannot begin to explain my longing to hold his hand, to look him in the eye, and to hear his sweet voice tell me he loves me. I talk to him. I talk to him nearly every night at around seven o'clock. I take medication to fall asleep. I need to sleep so that I can prepare to wake up in the morning and start again. My hope is that in time, everything that is different will eventually become familiar.

Here I am, I'm lying on my bed looking at the ceiling, and then I turn my eyes to the open closet. "Go ahead, brain, go nuts, think about a million things in the next sixty seconds; I can't stop you." The closet is missing his clothes, most of them anyway, and there's the word… "missing". Now, I will run with that word. "I miss you, Babe. I can't stand it, and I can't comprehend that you aren't laying right next to me." I must find a way to relieve my grief, so I use my imagination. Now, in my imagination, he is lying next to me. There, to my left (in my mind), he was just as he had been for years. I can't help myself; I reach over with my left hand, as I had done countless times. I needed to hold his hand, it was our thing, and I still need "our thing". I whisper, "Give me your hand, Babe." I tell myself a warrior mantra… "Cancer can take you from being here, but it can't take away my reaching for your hand, so I halfway win!" Ha! What a lie. I don't mind the lies, though; they are easier to handle than the truth. Small wins are HUGE in a grieving environment, in a grieving moment. I recommend that we acknowledge them.

It's been nine months, and I still get to reach for his hand. If you read that part and think I've lost my mind, you'd be right; welcome to my life. Please stay as long as you can brave it.

Chapter Eighteen
A Changeable Plan

People say "f*** cancer," and you don't really get the gravity of what they are saying until cancer destroys the life and love you became accustomed to. I say it because that's what took him, cancer; not God, not Jesus, not lack of optimism or a good attitude; cancer took him and the life we had. It took two people who were madly in love with each other, and it slowly and methodically grabbed our clasped hands and, with its unforgettable force, ripped our hands apart. Cancer doesn't realize, though, that it wasn't just our hands that were connected; our hearts were also connected, and they will always be. So, F*** you, cancer. You lose.

I tried every day to provide for his every need. When it was time, God took him home, and he no longer needed me. That feeling was confusing to me. I was no longer taking care of him, but he was still providing for me. His love sustains me through my grief, his financial plan takes care of me even today, and our memories tell me I was worthy of a man like him.

It's important for you and your partner to get your finances in order, your important documents signed, notarized, and in a safe place. If possible, have a plan for where you'll be in the weeks, months, and years after the loss of your spouse. You don't have to follow it all, but it's a great idea to have an idea to reduce confusion and the feeling of being so lost.

I read recently that widows in America get poorer as they age. I was told it's because people want them to deplete their assets before providing them with any help, but that makes no financial sense. In fact, it flies against the face of wisdom. Another thing to consider is that widows in their fifties and older often face age discrimination in the workplace, adding to the struggle of finding work that will cover their living costs.

Grieving is an intense way to exist. Expecting a stay-at-home wife to lose her husband and find a job quickly is a ridiculous expectation. You need time to grieve before taking on the task of finding a new job. Getting back into the workforce after being out of it for many years is no small feat. For me, I am legally disabled but was not allowed to get paid for six months after Larry's passing. Shock support is a kind of support a couple receives when their spouse is diagnosed with terminal cancer, but once they pass, the shock support goes away. It is understandable why people give at the news of the diagnosis. It's also understandable that people can't give at that same level for long periods of time. Prepare for that.

I had little to no money coming in for six months, and I needed to figure out where I was going to live. Larry and I were paying rent in the little beach apartment, but that was no longer affordable for me because I had no income. Once my income started, in six months, I still wouldn't have enough to stay in California. So, I left that beach house, and I spent 3 months in Oregon. Looking back, I believe I was on a healing trip. I had sheltered with dear friends in Oregon for as long as I needed. It was awesome because this family had begun offering their home to me *and* Larry well before Larry's passing. In my trauma and heartache, I had forgotten about their offer. They reached out to me for a third time, a couple of months after he passed away. They said they WANTED me to live with them. It was SUCH a God thing. God knows I didn't want to live anywhere where I wasn't wanted, and I had no income, so it had to be free. Sometimes, God does "free" stuff. He's not all about money. And God is *always* about the heart. I needed (in my heart) to feel wanted.

It was December 13[th,] and time to leave that little beach apartment. My tribe showed up to pack a U-Haul truck. Then, a full-on car challenge occurred: I had come to realize that my vehicle had a gas leak as there were dark spots in my driveway that smelled like gasoline. It was the day my friends showed up to load the truck. For the third time, I took my car to the local KIA dealership to tell them that the "check engine" light was still on. I advised them that my friends and family were loading my moving truck, as I was leaving for Oregon in a couple of hours, and would they check again to make sure I was safe to drive the car. The service department knew me and was aware of my husband's recent passing. Five hours after bringing my car to the service department, and after the U-Haul had driven away with my belongings in it, I was told I could not drive my car. The service advisor said that the recall they had done on it a month earlier was done with a faulty part, and they needed to order a new one. The new part would take two to three days to arrive. My friend, Kevin, had flown in from Vancouver, Canada, to help load the truck and then drive it to Oregon for me. But he also has a life, and he needed to be on his flight back to Canada just two days later. I felt I had no choice but to buy a different car and trade that one in. I purchased the only similar car and got a fair trade for my old car. I felt frustrated that I had to buy a car due to the company putting on a faulty part. This cost me an unexpected fifteen thousand dollars. I was not (and still am not) prepared financially for this setback. With the help of my sister, Traci, and my dear friend, Alicia, we moved my stuff into the newer model Kia Sorento. On I went, driving over the I-5 grade as giant tumbleweeds whisked across the dark rainy highway between my car and the semi-trucks that surrounded me. It was an eerie drive, to say the least. Several hours later, I finally caught up with Kevin at our first stop, somewhere in Northern California. My mind is now fully distracted, and while my stress levels are off the charts, it's a welcomed distraction from the grief.

We made it to Portland, Oregon. I checked into a hotel room near the airport so Kevin could get up at 4am to catch his flight. There I was, waking up at 7am, alone in an airport hotel. On my second morning there, I looked out the window and noticed giant flakes of snow falling from the sky, a stark contrast to the sunny beach property I had left three days ago. What a metaphor for my life right now. Am I running away from the agony of watching my husband suffer the ailments of metastatic lung cancer, or am I running into a life that will refuse my desire to be blanketed in the memories of our hometown? I'm not sure, but there's no stopping me now. I'm putting one foot in front of the other, begging anyone to help me make life's decisions, decisions ranging from what to order at Starbucks to where I should live. I have no idea what I'm doing, and I am keenly aware of that truth. I would spend a week in that airport hotel alone. It was very difficult.

On December 21st, I was able to check into my Airbnb in a nice area of Portland. I had arranged this stay well ahead of time. I wanted to spend my birthday and Christmas with my son, who lived in Portland with his fiancé; it was so nice: My son came over, brought me a cake AND candles; he sang the "Happy Birthday" song to me, and we watched the latest Matrix movie. We didn't care that the movie was a disappointment, only that we were together, and I didn't need to be alone on this, my first birthday without my love. Since my birthday is December 22, I had the joy of having my son and his fiancé over for Christmas too. These two and our pups got me through my first Christmas and birthday without Larry. I remember thinking…"I survived. I am alive! I made it!" I could never express my intense gratitude for them being there for me during that time.

Due to a snowstorm, I was stranded at that Portland Airbnb for three extra days, though longing desperately to leave. Another challenge I faced was that the house I was moving into in Salem, Oregon (one hour south) was not going to be available for a couple of weeks due to Covid. So, I was in Oregon with no place to go. I found another Airbnb along the Oregon coast and made my way to this single-wide trailer near the ocean. The location was fantastic, but the trailer was just…ugh… scary. A windstorm knocked out the power and internet service. I had no phone service, no heat, and no way to know where I should drive next. I loaded up my dog and my belongings when the morning light came, and I drove north until I had phone service. Not knowing where to go, I made it through a snowy forested highway to arrive in Portland. I found a random hotel in downtown Portland and checked in. At this point, my head was spinning like the grief-stricken, lost wife I had become. With no idea when I could move into my friend's house, I was spending money fast, money that I needed for my future. Finally, the house in Salem became available. I made my way there in the dark and pouring rain. I know what you might be thinking… "is this dark and pouring rain a theme?" I know, right? It seemed like every time I was making a big move, the rain came down, and the sky was dark. Here's a recap: Leaving Southern California, I faced a dark and stormy night with massive tumbleweeds, the moving company didn't show up to unload the truck into the storage unit and so Kevin and I ended up unloading the moving truck in Salem…in the dark and in the rain, and arriving at the Salem house ended up happening at night… in the rain.

Eventually, I decided to look at housing options in Oklahoma, near my daughter and grandkids. I knew I needed to be near either my son or my daughter. I ended up finding a house in a small town called Perry, located in Oklahoma. Perry is about 30 miles from Oklahoma State University. I fell in love with the house online, but I couldn't get to Perry to view it in person. I had an agent do a video walk-through, and I paid for an inspection to protect this purchase. This house checked all the boxes of what I asked God for. Unfortunately, once I got settled into the house, the pipes busted at the main, and I learned a rough lesson. Real Estate Agents place false information in ads that read "all plumbing is up to code" and "updates are already done". This leads people to think that pipes and electrical wiring are up to date, which in my case wasn't true. There I was, stuck paying for new plumbing. Yes, I contacted a real estate lawyer who said I have a case, but it would cost 40K to litigate it. He suggested that I contact the selling agent and request for them to pay for it. I contacted her, and she told me three times she was going to respond, but she never did.

I'm sharing this with you because some of you reading this are widows looking for homes. Let this be a "buyer beware" moment. I didn't really have anyone looking out for me while buying this house, but I do know that God will continue to provide for me. No matter what mankind does, please know that God will always send someone or equip you to handle your situations. I forgave the agent and left it in God's hands.

I've been in my house for one month, and in that time, I have had to replace the underground pipes, call the air conditioner company three times, get new gutters put on, turn off faulty electrical wiring, and fix the falling pillars under the house. All that said, I know this is the place for me.

There will always be people out there who do the wrong thing, and some will try to take advantage of you as a widow. Don't think that being a widow will cause people to be fair, some will, but many won't. Be ready for that and get extra help with your buying process and other changes you go through. There is help; keep asking if someone ignores you.

Chapter Nineteen
To the Caregiver

You are a rock star. Sadly, you are enduring something you never thought would exist in your life. You are carrying the weight of the world on your shoulders. None of this is fair. I see you: I see the nights without sleep, I see the worry, I see the frustration, I see the burden on your back, I see the fear in your eyes, I see the ambition to be the best you can be, I see the valiant warrior you are, I see the love in your heart, and the way it is intertwined with the ache, equally existing with every beat.

Rest is allowed. Asking for help is not a sign of weakness; it's a sign of strength. Take care of yourself by doing the things that make you calm; things like prayer, meditation, massage, exercise, morning or evening walks, and a dozen donuts, even if you only eat one. You need to do that which energizes you. Do the things that strengthen your resolve to take each day one hour at a time. Get on with your days using something I like to call an "eager calmness". Be eager to live and calm enough to make living your primary focus rather than dying.

To prepare you for later, I need to tell you what life might be like once your spouse is gone.

In your life, it feels like you are walking through fire, and I know it's hot, and I know it hurts like hell. You will get to the end of the fire, and then you'll walk on coals for a while. Most of the help you had during your spouse's cancer journey will stop after his or her funeral. Everyone will need to get on with their lives, and you'll feel lonely. Your heart will hurt more now than it did before, but that's because you loved so deeply the one that you lost.

I want you to know that many of the people you think have abandoned you are thinking of you; some are praying for you, and they don't understand your pain or loneliness because they can't understand it. No one is absent willingly. They don't know what to do now. Grace, in the face of their ignorance, is your new motto, and it will sustain you. Be gracious and see that none of the absence is out of malice or lack of love. Reach out and tell your friends you need sister/brother time, friend time, and help with whatever it is you need help with. If they don't answer, ask someone else. You have the right to ask for help…still.

Some will judge you. Some will say things like, "why doesn't she just get a job? Seriously, a new job will be a good distraction." Or "Why would she ask us for help and keep changing her plans?" Some will make judgments about your decisions without having a real conversation with you. Those people don't know anything about what you're going through. I learned a hard lesson, but at least I learned that walking away from negative people is not only okay but necessary for your health. Remember, you are on a healing journey now. You have no room in your life for anything but loving and kind responses to your suffering. Please move forward, and drop them from your life (for now). You need to heal from the acute pain that loss causes. It's time to focus on discovering what grieving means for you, specifically.

You will finally come to the realization that grief is not something you go through but something you learn to carry with you. It's not something you get over. I learned that instead of grief ending me, I could allow it to change me. I could harness its profound power to empower me. You can do this too.

Once your love is gone, slow down. Don't rush your days. Go at your own (new) pace while at the same time figuring out when to push yourself. My doctor told me that "Grief is a beast"; he's right. Grief wants to take you down, don't let it. Do the hard things: Go to lunch or dinner by yourself, go to the movies alone, or just try a bike ride. It's gonna be uncomfortable, and it will hurt at first but do it anyway. When you're ready to try whatever IT is… try it. If you drive a mile and need to go back home, you've done better than staying home. That's my advice... One foot in front of the other, as slow as you feel you need to go. Don't let anyone force you to do anything that you aren't comfortable doing. Ignore the ones telling you that you're doing it wrong. If you're not choosing unhealthy coping mechanisms, you're doing it right.

Just for fun, count the times someone tells you, "Don't make any important decisions for a year!" and compare that advice to how many times someone asks you, "So, what are you gonna do next?" That's when you'll discover that no one has this thing figured out. Finally, I truly believe that your help comes from the Lord...and HE LOVES THE WIDOW so, SO much. Trust this...He LOVES YOU!

Chapter Twenty
Advice for Friends & Family

If you know a widow who is brave enough to ask for your opinion, advice, or guidance, see it as that, brave. Don't see it as her asking for a handout. She's unsure of every move she is making. Don't assume that your dollars are what she's seeking; she knows everyone has given so much already. Sometimes, she's merely seeking light in the darkness. See her request for your advice as the raw truth that it is. It's really her wanting to know what YOU think. It might be hard to say what you think. Say it anyway, but say it in love. That's what she needs, and that's exactly what she's asking for. She knows she's not mentally well enough to navigate the world, as it has become too dark for her now. You, she hopes, might be one to hold a flashlight.

I want to desperately try to explain what the grieving brain is like. I think it's important to make this attempt for a few reasons: if more can even grasp it a little bit, they might judge less, the widow, who is unable to go back to the church where she attended with her spouse, maybe those who know her won't take personally her newfound zombie-like mentality. People may show her more compassion during the intense mourning she is experiencing. Maybe people will turn their focus on her needs more than their confusion as to why she is behaving oddly. I hope that the information I share here will help deepen love for the widowed and that those who love her will see her through the eyes of grace.

Mary-Frances O'Connor, Ph.D., wrote a profound, scientific book about grief. It's titled "The Grieving Brain". I'm going to spend a bit of time on this book because I believe it will enlighten you. It has helped me understand better why I am so different now.

In her book, Mary-Frances describes this idea of "the absence of something drawing our attention" she describes that as strange or weird; we typically think of "something drawing our attention". She provides a simple metaphor, using the furniture one skirts around in their home, in the middle of the night, on their way to get a drink of water; for years, they would bump the same table on their way to the sink, then suddenly, one night, no bumping, it is missing now. That simple missing of the normal, the typical, everyday sensation, interaction, and encounter is missing, and it is no longer drawing our attention. She describes so eloquently the concept of constantly trying to find our spouse, trying to see him or her where they were and why our brains do that. It's a brilliant read.

In this book, she goes on to talk a lot about the science of it all. So, let's talk more about science because it's so interesting to understand the why's of our brains in grief. A groundbreaking study performed by Norwegian Scientists Edward Moser and May-Britt Moser used mice to understand the brain and how it functions in a loss. For weeks, they had a mouse go into a box where they recorded the neuro firing in its brain. The only thing that was in that box was a tall, blue Lego block. Every time it went in the box, the brain's neurons fired on. Finally, after weeks of this, they removed the tall, blue block, but the neurons fired on in the mouse's brain for a long time after. They explain that this happens because the brain's map has been conditioned to encounter the object it had become so used to seeing that it still encountered it, even after the object was gone. This is something that happens with humans too. We are living in two realities, the past and the present, and trust me, I'm there now, and …it's a real "mind f..." sometimes. I mean, it can really make a person feel strange in this new existence they are unable to escape from. It's constantly confusing to live in two realities. Reality tv shows have become a clear entertainment hoax. We, the grieving ones, are the ones living in two alternate realities.

We can learn countless lessons about the science of the brain in grieving, but I'll leave that up to you to get that book. It will enlighten you. Before I completely drop the book's lessons, though, I want to tell you that it debunks the idea of the "stages of grief". The problem with a well-intended theory created some time ago is that those stages create an expectation. People are expected to be at a specific stage at a specific time. The people around the one grieving might feel confused when the one they love is not experiencing these stages the way they expected. There are, at times, more stages, fewer stages, and non-linear stages to the grieving person's life. Let go of your expectations of what you or the one you love is supposed to be going through.

Chapter Twenty-One
What to say/What not to say

If you've been in my shoes, you know that people mean well. I heard things like "At least you weren't married for a long time" and "Can you imagine how Queen Elizabeth feels, losing the love of her life after so many years together?" I wonder if they consider the fact that we are meant to grow old together, and one typically dies before the other. The goal IS to grow old and pass away. The goal IS to spend many, many years together. My only response to these types of statements is, "I'm sure she is so sad." But, in my mind, it looks more like this: "Can you imagine how I feel? If only I had fifty years with the love of my life, and not the mere 8 years, five months, and 18 days." I wonder if Queen Elizabeth counted the days from her first date with her husband, then I slowly back out of this minefield of comparison and move on with my day.

What not to say? Nothing to delineate the grieving heart of another person. Nothing that gives a description or boxes it in. Nothing that places any comparison on it. Saying things like "I can't imagine" work well because while it says the word "imagine" in it, a sane person doesn't imagine this, but what that phrase is saying is "I cannot understand your pain, but I'm here if I can help with anything at all." Saying things like "Please know that I think of you often" and then back that up with an action, something like sending flowers, a gift card, or an audible book subscription can be helpful.

If you want an idea of what to say DURING the cancer fight itself, I can only tell you from our experience, but that's the point of this book, so here it is...SAY less than you DO. Less advice on alternative options to cure the cancer and more offers to clean the house, give rides, raise money, pharmacy or supermarket runs, car maintenance issues like oil changes, DoorDash gift cards, any gift cards, phone calls, pet care, taking kids to appointments, get an attorney to handle financial issues, send a financial advisor to help the couple make decisions, offer counseling sessions, lawn mowing, and maybe even set up an Amazon wish list online. These are some ideas. Ask the person to make a list and try to get a team together to see if they can help. The fight and aftermath are utterly time-consuming, money-sucking, and physically exhausting. Doing something to help is... well... helpful.

Chapter Twenty-Two
Collateral Beauty

Everything I see that was once beautiful is now extraordinary. Every vibrant green tree, every blue sky, every sunflower and rose were more vibrant than before. I watched this movie the day before my 55th birthday, the first without him. The movie was called "Collateral Beauty," and it moved me today. I see how love is all of this: it's holding his hand, hugging him, watching him take his last breath with me by his side, and finally…it's missing him this much, which is a whole lot. Love is powerful and intertwined with pain. I'll miss him, but I won't miss him forever. I'll miss him until I see him again. I'll miss him a lot because I love him a lot and love is a beautiful thing. We, as humans, need to hurt powerfully in order to love powerfully, and we must always desire to love powerfully.

Chapter Twenty-Three
The Widow & The Church

Many churches in America are missing the mark when it comes to caring for their community's widows. In my attempt to try to understand why my church (minus four women) abandoned me after my husband's memorial service, I joined several online widows support groups. I wanted to know if it was just my church or if it was an epidemic that exists within the American church culture. This chapter will be hard for church leaders to read; some won't bother, but I hope if that's you, and you've gotten this far, that you will humble yourself and hear what I believe God wants to say to the church of today, as it relates to widows.

Fifty percent of widows leave their church, according to Pat Brandenstein of Encore Ministries. Brandenstein wrote in an article about some of the reasons widows find it difficult to go back to the church where they attended alongside their husbands; some are: 1-They feel like a bride walking down the aisle, and all eyes are on them, 2-They wonder if they will sit where their husband sat with them not long ago and 3-They are wondering if they are going to cry. For me, I wondered if I would completely lose it in public during worship where my husband was no longer on stage, but instead, someone else was now leading, someone whom I didn't know at all. Would that void destroy me as I stood there? Would I be able to sit and listen to a teacher who I had lost respect for... and then would I take it out on God? I didn't want to suffer any more than I was already suffering. Brandenstein writes, "we need to be aware of how each widow is feeling and how we can assist her in returning to church." You can read more about Brandonstein's article and whom this ministry considers to be widows by going to encoureministries.org's website.

In an article dated July 21, 2021, Jill Foley Turner wrote, "In a way, we are all widows". Anyone who is "bereft" deserves the kind of care God commands for widows. Andy explains that women of *any* age may have lost their husbands in varying ways. He says, "This is a large population of our churches. Single mothers are widows, and their children are fatherless." But it's not just them.

After spending a literal quarter century in James 1:27, Andy says he can see the whole gospel in it. "It's the most challenging passage in Scripture for me." It's true religion to serve widows and orphans because their condition is *our* condition apart from Jesus, he explains. Since Adam and Eve after the garden, it has been so. Without Jesus, we're worse than at risk. We are without protection – husbandless and fatherless.

Before I wrote this chapter, I wanted to give my old church a chance to explain why the elders abandoned me after my husband's funeral. I asked the pastor directly if it was because of the teaching in 1 Timothy 5. I was told it was because of that teaching because they felt I should have used my retirement money before asking for help, AND because I offended them by a couple of Facebook posts, posts where I mentioned churches (in America) abandoning widows. My church, and many churches in America, use the following scripture to dismiss a widow's needs; financial and otherwise...

1 Timothy 5:3-15

3 Give proper recognition to those widows who are really in need. **4** But if a widow has children or grandchildren, these should learn first of all to put their religion into practice by caring for their own family and so repaying their parents and grandparents, for this is pleasing to God. **5** The widow who is really in need and left all alone puts her hope in God and continues night and day to pray and to ask God for help. **6** But the widow who lives for pleasure is dead even while she lives. **7** Give the people these instructions, so that no one may be open to blame. **8** Anyone who does not provide for their relatives, and especially for their own household, has denied the faith and is worse than an unbeliever.

9 No widow may be put on the list of widows unless she is over sixty, has been faithful to her husband, 10 and is well known for her good deeds, such as bringing up children, showing hospitality, washing the feet of the Lord's people, helping those in trouble and devoting herself to all kinds of good deeds.

11 As for younger widows, do not put them on such a list. For when their sensual desires overcome their dedication to Christ, they want to marry. 12 Thus they bring judgment on themselves, because they have broken their first pledge. 13 Besides, they get into the habit of being idle and going about from house to house. And not only do they become idlers, but also busybodies who talk nonsense, saying things they ought not to. 14 So I counsel younger widows to marry, to have children, to manage their homes and to give the enemy no opportunity for slander. 15 Some have in fact already turned away to follow Satan." (biblegateway.com)

At this point, I have caused some women's (and even men's) blood to boil. Ignoring my requests for help with moving, packing, meals, and to continue the ministry opportunity we had been doing is certainly preposterous. As my ex-pastor emailed me with these as the reasons, stating, "You aren't sixty, are you?" I had to ask myself if he (and the elders) considered the text within the context it was written. The reason Paul used the age "over 60" is because he is saying that younger women (women under 60) can remarry and have children. I am a disabled woman. I am fifty-five years of age. So no, I'm not 60. I am, however, fully devoted to Christ, unable to have more children, have teenage grandchildren, and I am not desiring to remarry.

It's important to note (so I am not viewed as a lazy woman) that I began seeking work while my husband was sick, and I was taking care of him but was unable to secure employment. The government declared me permanently disabled due to Systemic

Lupus, Gastroparesis, and severe anxiety and depression, which worsened due to my husband's passing. The pain I endured in the aftermath of everything we went through is impossible to quantify.

When Timothy says a woman who loses her husband should be supported by her family, he is talking about family with resources who are also followers of Christ. My family did not have the resources, and most were not followers of Christ.

When the church said, "no," God said, "YES!" With that "yes", Larry's family, Kevin, my friends in Oregon, my girlfriends, my sister, and my children all did what they could to help me. Make no mistake, Jesus LOVES the widow, even when the church gets it wrong. God is faithful and ALWAYS gets it right.

What does "love" look like in your church? Does it match how Jesus defines love? Does it match how Jesus defines true religion?

Below is a more in-depth, personal account of how my specific church dealt with me. It is not meant to indict them but to help any church that is humble enough to hear this message to treat their widows with love and compassion. If I had not been so in love and devoted to Christ when Larry passed away, my elder's absence from my life after his memorial service would have been enough to push me to suicide. It was that hurtful; if this is you, hold on; Hope exists, and it's yours for the taking. Jesus is your Jireh, your provider. For me...I was made to feel unimportant, greedy, needy, and opportunistic. The reality is that I was lost, confused, lonely, and seeking guidance in every direction. I couldn't make decisions such as: when to take a shower, how to manage day-to-day finances, where I was going to live, what kind of future I needed to plan for, and how to make the little amount of money we set aside for my future last for the remainder of my life. We had a small life insurance policy which was kept with a financial advisor strictly for the use of buying a house, an agreement I made with Larry. As a disabled 55yr old woman, I had to consider my financial needs for many years to come. I wasn't young, but I wasn't old either.

My pastor told me that the church's elders felt they shouldn't help me with meals after the memorial or with moving costs or manpower to load my truck because I had a little bit of money left in our IRA and a small amount of money to buy a house. They felt that I should have depleted those funds before they should help me.

When Larry was here, we had a monthly income, either through his company or through Social Security; the day Larry passed, my income stopped. Our rent was $1600 per month. I had paid rent for three months after his passing, and his brother let me stay there for a month at no charge. Larry's sister, brother, and Kevin took very good care of me. Together, these three made sure I had food, gas, and money to pay my bills. Some of those bills were Larry's, some were mine, and some were both of ours.

It's important for me to explain here what I asked for from the church where my husband was the worship pastor and an elder and explain each one. I asked for three things: 1-Moving help. 2-Meals after the memorial had come and gone and 3-To continue (for a little while) doing the ministry Larry and I had been doing.

My requests for help with moving were ignored completely by the elder, who said he would get back to me, then never did. I had three very sweet ladies from the church show up to help me pack. I love them deeply and will always be grateful for their help in that process. Not one man showed up to help load the truck, no one offered to help hire movers, and not one elder even explained why they were ignoring my text message and phone calls. I learned much later that they were offended by Facebook posts, and that was why.

I asked for help with meals early on because that is normal when someone passes. I had heard it is common for a church to provide meals to a widow when a spouse passes, so when the pastor texted to check on me, that sounded like something I could use for a while. I had a huge issue going to the grocery store because I'd emotionally break down and cry. To that request, they simply ignored me.

Larry and I had begun reading scripture which we recorded for the church. They would play the recording before a message was given. When I asked if I could keep doing the ministry of reading scripture before a sermon was done, I was told, "no, that was only for Larry". Later I was told by the pastor that my request to continue reading after his passing was "odd" to him. He said he felt that way because I had not been to the church (which was an hour away) in person since Larry's passing. I believe the correct response would have been to let me keep reading the scriptures if for no other reason, to help me stay involved during my mourning period. I believe my request should have been thought of as brave, not "odd".

Larry and I served this church behind the scenes in ways that cannot be made public, but we ministered to a specific church leader from Larry's diagnosis to while literally on his death bed. Finally, the last lunch meeting with a church member revealed my time there was done. It would be gossip and hurtful to go into those details, but after talking with two therapists in-depth, I was advised to leave this church. I was told, and I agreed that God was taking me away from this church. I knew too much negative information to be there any longer. While some criticized me for not returning to that church, I will never be able to share the reasons why; I know that Jesus is fully aware of it all. I trust that His work is being done in those who hurt me, but I also pray that God will work on me too. In the healing process, I have forgiven those who so easily judged me.

There are thousands upon thousands of widows in our country who are being treated as non-widows due to poor teaching and a lack of basic love and compassion. I would like to propose a new approach to helping the widows in your church, including a widow who has been dependent on her husband, a widow who has not been dependent, a widow who is young and a widow who is old, a widow who is disabled, like me, and a widow who is abled. Stop saying she isn't a widow because that is not true. Stand alongside your widows and give them grace. If she posts something online that hurts your feelings, go to her, and do it immediately.

I am grateful for God's provision through this church before Larry's passing. I am grateful to my Lord because He cared for me after his passing, using strangers, friends, other churches, as well as both mine and Larry's family.

A young couple, who were dear friends of mine, invited me to live with them in Oregon. They had no stipulations, no requirements. They wanted me to just be there and heal with no time restraints. It was this couple, a whole bunch of Christian brothers and sisters, my family and my best friends, and yes, at times, even strangers, who saw me for who I am...a 55yr old disabled woman and a widow, worthy of being loved, protected and advised.

My life has been flipped upside down. I never wanted to move back to the Midwest, but I am here, and I believe this is where God wants me. I took financial advice from a dear friend, advice that helped me make this move halfway across the United States. It's a good thing that I didn't spend the small amount of money that Larry stipulated for me to buy a house. If I had used that money as liquid cash, I would not have been able to afford the house I'm living in today.

I chose this town because I knew that I needed to be near one of my children; as I said earlier, my son is in Oregon, but my daughter, her husband, and my grandchildren live here in Oklahoma. Oregon's real estate market was too expensive for me, but the Oklahoma market was something I could manage. It's wonderful being near my grandchildren. My daughter and I deserve more time together, but that's another story. I'm happy to be so close to them now.

Church leadership really must focus on ways to love the widow. Their widows need pragmatic help. Grace for the widow is a conversation for elders and all church leadership to have. I was told by my old pastor that my church's leadership got offended by a Facebook post I made. The post talked about how the church in America abandons its widows. I was told that because of that post, "people threw up their hands" when it came to me. I was told that the social media post was the reason they ignored my three requests for help with loading my moving truck.

Thanks to a small church in Salem, Oregon, people I had never met before loaded my moving truck. I drove that Penske truck across five states, towing my car. When I pulled up to my new 1920s craftsman house, I was met by my new church's congregation. These people had never met me, but they showed up to unload my truck. God is faithful to provide.

Chapter Twenty-Four
Let's Do Better

Over fifty percent of widows leave their church. There are varying reasons why this happens. In my support groups, I often hear the stories of church abandonment; it baffles me. My story is one of many. While my church was very hands-on during the fight, the leadership stopped supporting me in the aftermath. Nine months later, I learned why. I was told that because I did not go back to church after Larry passed away, people felt slighted. A couple of months after Larry passed away, I was told that my not going back (to at least extend my gratitude) would leave a "bad taste in people's mouths". In response to this, I created a "Thank you" video to be played for the church. I was told they would play that video after Christmas, though I'm not sure if they did or not.

I know for a fact that the elders at my church have huge hearts and are men of great integrity. I needed them to meet me where I was in my grief. I needed them to not judge my inability to go back to church after watching my husband take his last breath. I needed their guidance to help direct me. It feels sad that they didn't feel they could. I am still confused by their absence. It just wasn't like them. I believe I made mistakes in how I handled my shock at their absence, but I also believe a person in mourning requires a great amount of grace. It is important here to mention that four of the ladies in that church never stopped being there for me. I still feel their love today.

BUT GOD! God sent help through other friends and family. He also sent a therapist who would become not only my counselor but my friend. This is powerful because it reveals something important, something we all need to remember. NEVER let the actions of mankind determine your opinion of God. Sometimes the actions of man prove our need for God; sometimes, the actions of man reveal there is a God. Either way, we need Jesus.

As I reflect on the love, life, and death we experienced as a couple, I can say that we were, and I am now, very blessed. The thing about it all is this; we loved truly, we forgave powerfully, and we fought valiantly. I am, by the grace of God, enduring bravely. We never did any of this alone, even when we, or I, felt drawn to loneliness; God never allowed it. He always made sure WE had support, and then... that I had support.

Today, I am building a widow's ministry in the town I live in. I am working with "Stand in the Gap Ministries" and Perry Assembly of God to build this ministry here in the Midwest. My goal is to help churches know how to help their widows. So often, the reason widows get forgotten is because churches don't know how to help. I want God to use me to change that.

Finally, please let me end with this: I miss you, babe. When my work here is done, I will see you again. This life is but a blink, and eternity means never having to say... "I'll see you soon".